infuse

OIL, SPIRIT, WATER

ERIC PRUM & JOSH WILLIAMS

CLARKSON POTTER/PUBLISHERS

NEW YORK

foreword

by
elizabeth tilton

During my time at the University of Virginia, a friend introduced me to Josh and Eric. Beyond a friendship that immediately blossomed over glasses of bourbon, a partnership among the three of us started to brew in the kitchen. When we met, Josh and Eric had just begun a catering company. Having recently created a catering venture of my own, I began working with them and started cooking for events from central Virginia to Washington, D.C. Josh and Eric focused their expertise on savories while I did desserts. It was a match made in heaven.

Catering with the guys taught me two major lessons. The first: If you commit to a 400-person party as your very first catering gig, ask for help (oh and try not to light your oven on fire halfway through the night). The second: Three individuals could come together to produce something greater than the sum of the individual contributions.

Infuse: Oil, Spirit, Water embodies this second point. As a trained pastry cook, I learned that there are many occasions when a list of recipe ingredients can seem disjointed at first glance, but, when combined, these seemingly disparate elements can create something completely new and more complex. Josh and Eric have put together a book filled with recipes that transform simple, fresh ingredients into unique infusions that will help you develop and expand the depth of flavors in your own kitchen.

Infuse complements Josh and Eric's cocktail knowledge showcased in their first full-length book, *Shake: A New Perspective on Cocktails*, and highlights their understanding and passion for the culinary world outside of the cocktail glass. So pick up a few Mason jars and get to work. It is amazing what inspired ingredients and a bit of time can produce.

Elizabeth Tilton is professionally trained in pastry and has cooked at Sucré and Restaurant August in New Orleans, among other places. She is on the public relations and marketing team at Momofuku in NYC.

eric

josh

introduction

The story behind *Infuse* begins one summer nearly a decade ago, the day we first made peach bourbon. We were awestruck. The combination of two basic ingredients, eight-year-old Kentucky bourbon and fresh, local peaches—and a handful of weeks had resulted in an amazing peach-infused bourbon that we couldn't get enough of.

It seemed like alchemy, being able to transform two simple ingredients into such an utterly delicious new substance. The moment we tasted that liquid gold we knew we wanted to share this feeling of creative joy with others. Over the coming years we started incorporating infusions into our everyday cooking and entertaining, until it became second nature. Whether it was a spicy chili oil drizzled over homemade pasta, a Mason jar of roasted pineapple-infused mezcal passed around a "Friendsgiving" party, or a citrus-infused water stored in the fridge for an especially hot day, we couldn't resist the 1+1=3 magic of infusions.

Infuse is the result of all those delightful experiments and a few more we've tinkered with at our Brooklyn workshop. Although spirits have always been our game, we've found that great infusions can derive from a variety of liquids. In this book, you'll find three main types as we see them: oils, spirits, and waters. All three liquids have distinct characteristics that influence infusing times, temperatures, and ingredients, and all are equally exciting to us.

Our hope is that *Infuse* inspires you to pick up some fresh ingredients and to experiment with your own infusions. If you experience anything close to the joy we felt that day so many years ago, jars full of peach bourbon and smiles on our faces, well, we'll have succeeded in our mission.

eric & josh

table of contents

We cover the fundamentals of how we infuse, including the tools we stock at home, the types of liquids you can use for infusions, the kinds of ingredients out there, and the role time plays in getting the flavors you're after.

Oil infusions present salty, spicy, and herbaceous flavor possibilities. Infused oils can elevate any everyday dish, whether it's a grilled pizza finished with chili oil from the spicy southern tip of Italy or a basic salad tossed with our essential vinaigrette (which we guarantee will upgrade your salads for all time).

As cocktail guys, we're especially fond of infused spirits. Alcohol can be used in a wide variety of infusions, so we offer up our very favorite techniques and recipes: flash-infusing spirits with farmer's market produce, crafting our version of a classic Italian liqueur, and creating the perfect Bloody Mary base that we keep on hand for whenever the mood strikes.

Though it doesn't often get the credit it deserves, water is the most versatile liquid for infusions. We use this Swiss Army knife of a medium to make everything from cooling cucumber mint water, to soda syrup infused with sea salt and lime, to our take on a Vietnamese cold-brewed coffee. Read on, and get thirsty.

the basics

In this section we cover the fundamentals of how we create infusions, including the tools we stock at home, the types of liquids used for infusions, the kinds of flavoring ingredients out there, and the role time plays in getting the flavors you're after. In other words, everything you need to get started.

a.

b.

c.

d.

e.

tools

a. Muddler: A muddler will break down ingredients and speed the release of flavors into your base liquid. By crushing or bruising ingredients, you remove the physical barriers containing the flavors within.

b. Funnel: A funnel is a crucial piece of equipment for transferring infusions from one container to another without making a complete mess. We like to use a high-quality stainless steel funnel that's easy to clean and won't carry over flavors from one infusion to the next.

c. Strainer: A mesh strainer is the first level of filtering for your infusions. For the second and finer type, see cheesecloth below. A fine mesh strainer will remove any large pieces of flavoring ingredients from your infusion, increasing clarity and shelf life.

d. Peeler: A good peeler does everything from remove a fine layer of zest from a fresh grapefruit (while leaving behind the bitter white pith) to peel a cucumber. Don't bother with anything fancy; the simpler, the better.

e. Cheesecloth: When you are making an infusion that has fine particles of ground ingredients you should always use cheesecloth in addition to a fine mesh strainer. It provides a finer layer of straining, removing grit or other fine particles from your final product, like The Hanoi Cold Brew (page 139) or flash-infused oils (page 44).

mason jars

Long before they became a trend, Mason jars served a simple but crucial function in the home: preserving food. These durable, heat-resistant vessels are the perfect container for infusing and storing your finished infusions. The glass makes cleaning and reusing the jars easy and prevents lingering flavors from prior infusions.

We use three sizes of Mason jars for our infusions: 8 oz for precious batches of potent infusions used in small quantities (like infused oils), 16 oz for infusions that we use in slightly larger quantities (like infused spirits), and 32 oz for infusions that are served in large portions (like infused waters).

8 oz
(cup)

16 oz
(pint)

32 oz
(quart)

the mason tap

Not long ago, we found ourselves with Mason jars full of all these delicious infusions, and no way of pouring them without spilling all over ourselves (and our guests). To avoid any more costly plaid shirt replacements, we designed a stainless steel infuser top that attaches to any regular-mouth Mason jar, allowing you to infuse and dispense neatly. We call it the Mason Tap.

Stainless steel

Flip cap lid

Fits any regular-mouth Mason jar

15

base liquids

Oil, spirits, and water are the three base liquids we most love to infuse. As each of these liquids has its own unique infusing technique, we've divided *Infuse* into three sections.

oil

Given the high viscosity of oil, the infusion process for oils often requires a bit of physical effort. You'll need to cut, muddle, and shake the flavoring ingredients with the thick oil to coax out the flavors. A little effort goes a long way, though: Oil also acts as a preservative. By protecting the ingredients from outside air, many of our oil infusions will last, sealed, for long periods of time.

spirit

Spirits are efficient (and delicious) base liquids for infusions. Alcohol accelerates the extraction of flavors from ingredients, resulting in short infusing times and tasty infusions. The possibilities for spirit infusions abound and include everything from homemade liqueurs to flash-infused flavored spirits. Similar to oils, the alcohol in spirits acts as a preserving agent, adding to the lifespan of your concoctions.

water

Water pairs best with fresh ingredients such as fruit, herbs, and even vegetables to create flavored waters and cold-brewed iced teas. Water infusions generally have a shorter shelf life than oil and spirit infusions, as water doesn't act as a preservative like the other liquids. Because of this, infused waters should generally be kept refrigerated and enjoyed soon after being prepared.

17

ingredients

fresh

dried

Two types of ingredients are used in infusions: fresh and dried. Each produces different flavors in the infusing process. Using fresh ingredients like mint sprigs, strawberries, or cucumber slices produces bright, punchy, high notes for your infusion. On the other hand, dried ingredients such as lavender, tea leaves, and coffee can produce richer, more subtle flavor profiles in the finished product. We sometimes use both fresh and dried ingredients in our infusions to create a balance of flavors that hit on multiple levels, such as in our cold-brewed teas (page 148), which combine the deep flavors of dried tea leaves with the fresh notes of seasonal fruit.

time

Time is one of the most important factors in making infusions. When you choose to stop the infusing process determines the level and types of flavors you'll taste in the final product. We see three basic categories of infusions, broken down by time:

I. / immediate

An immediate infusion is just that: a recipe you can enjoy right after you prepare it.

II. / short

A short infusion takes up to 24 hours to allow the flavors to develop.

III. / long

A long infusion can take anywhere from one day to a few weeks to allow the ingredients to fully infuse in the base liquid.

oil

Infused oils are a great way to elevate casual meals by adding layers of flavor to everyday recipes. We incorporate infused oils into our day-to-day cooking in a variety of ways, such as a slow-infused Calabrian chili oil (page 25) topping smoky grilled pizza (page 26), a simple vinaigrette (page 30) tossed with crisp snap peas and fresh green herbs (page 35), or a freshly infused basil oil (page 49) finishing off a summer salad of heirloom tomatoes (page 51). We've also been known to combine some of these infused oils and dishes with good friends and plenty of sunshine on our rooftop during the warm Brooklyn summer for an Italian-inspired grilled meal (page 56), capped off with a few sips of homemade limoncello.

Calabrian
Chili Peppers

Extra Virgin
Olive Oil

Chili Peppers

Calabrian

grinding dried Italian chilies produces a powerful and
flavorful spice in this slow-infused chili oil

Olio Santo

spicy Calabrian chili oil

⏱ *2 weeks* 🥛 *8 oz*

1/2 oz of dried Calabrian chilies

8 oz of extra virgin olive oil

---

i.   Grind the chilies in a spice grinder or food processor until coarsely ground (use gloves or wash your hands after handling!).

ii. Combine with the olive oil in an 8 oz Mason jar. Seal and shake briefly until the ground chilies are evenly mixed into the oil.

iii. Let sit in a cool, dark place for two weeks to allow the oil to infuse and the chilies to settle.

iv. Use sparingly as you would use hot sauce. The infusion will keep for up to two months stored in a cool, dark place.

Great for grilled pizza (turn the page for a recipe combining ricotta, honey, and Olio Santo) and homemade pasta, and for elevating weeknight delivery pizza.

Calabria, the southernmost region of mainland Italy, produces some of the spiciest food in the country, including this slow-infused chili oil called Olio Santo. We keep this around all year, adding drops of flavorful heat to any dish that needs a bit of kick. If you can't find Calabrian chilies, you can substitute your favorite type of spicy dried chili.

spicy.

---

separation anxiety?

A little space can be a good thing. The ground chilies will separate from the oil and sink to the bottom of the jar over time. Stay calm! This is a good thing, allowing you to easily pour off the clear chili oil on the top.

Grilled
Pizza
Bianca

with Olio Santo

 Serves 4

This grilled white pizza combines a crispy, chewy, and smoky crust with creamy sheep's milk ricotta, floral honey, and spicy Olio Santo to create an irresistible starter for an outdoor grilling session.

8 oz of fresh pizza dough

2 tablespoons of olive oil

Sea salt flakes

Freshly ground black pepper

1/2 cup of sheep's milk ricotta (whipped with a whisk until creamy)

1/4 cup of chives (cut into batons)

1/4 cup of wildflower honey

Olio Santo (page 25)

---

i. Form the pizza dough into a ball and let rest for 10 minutes.

ii. Preheat a grill to high heat. Stretch the pizza dough into a long rectangle approximately 18 inches by 6 inches. Brush with olive oil and season with a pinch each of salt and pepper.

iii. Brush the grill grates with olive oil, then put on the pizza dough, stretching it into shape as you place it on the grill.

iv. Cover and grill until blistered and crisp (a little char is a good thing), then flip and repeat on the other side.

v. Remove the pizza from the grill and top with ricotta, chives, and salt and pepper. Drizzle honey evenly over the pizza and finish with Olio Santo to taste.

---

don't have the time?

While we love good homemade pizza dough, it takes a long time to make. Take a shortcut for this recipe and swing by your local pizzeria: They will more than likely sell you some of their dough, ready to throw on the grill.

the **perfect**
simple
vinaigrette

Homemade salad dressing, like most things, is best kept to the basics. Here to prove that point is the perfect simple vinaigrette, an easy-to-follow no-fail formula for delicious salad dressing. We start by making a base for the vinaigrette, combining a standard ratio of oil and vinegar with good sea salt and freshly ground pepper. While you could stop right there, shake to emulsify, and enjoy your work, we often will toss in an accent flavor to customize the vinaigrette to the salad we are making. Who knew homemade dressings could be that easy?

the base

4 Parts Oil

1 Part Vinegar

Sea Salt and Pepper

The method for making the perfect simple vinaigrette begins by creating a base dressing, following an easy formula. To start, add 1 part of your chosen vinegar to an 8 oz Mason jar. Add sea salt and freshly ground black pepper to taste. Seal the jar and shake until the salt is fully dissolved in the vinegar. Uncap the jar and add 4 parts of your chosen oil to complete the base dressing. From here, you can add flavoring ingredients (such as fresh herbs), reseal the jar, and shake until emulsified.

The Mason jar's sealable lid and small size allows for easy shaking—no whisking or blending required—and it makes storing the finished vinaigrette a breeze.

our recipes

The Essential

The Greek

The Orchard

The Spaniard

These are a few of our favorite dressings to make using the basic vinaigrette technique. Don't be afraid to mix it up and try variations of your own, substituting your favorite oils, vinegars, herbs, and spices. Vinaigrettes will keep in the refrigerator for up to one week.

The Essential 🥛 *5 oz*

Great for tossing with a snap pea and herb salad (turn the page for the recipe) and just about any other leafy greens you throw its way.

2 tablespoons of champagne vinegar

1/2 teaspoon of sea salt

1/8 teaspoon of freshly ground black pepper

4 tablespoons of olive oil

4 tablespoons of canola oil

i.   Combine all ingredients except oils in an 8 oz Mason jar.

ii.   Seal and shake for 30 seconds.

iii.   Add oils, seal, and shake for 30 seconds more.

The Orchard 🥛 *5 oz*

We love to use this vinaigrette to dress a hearty cool-weather kale and apple salad (turn the page for the recipe).

2 tablespoons of apple cider vinegar

1/2 teaspoon of honey

1/2 teaspoon of sea salt

1/8 teaspoon of freshly ground black pepper

4 tablespoons of walnut oil

4 tablespoons of canola oil

i.   Combine all ingredients except oils in an 8 oz Mason jar.

ii.   Seal and shake for 30 seconds.

iii.   Add oils, seal, and shake for 30 seconds more.

The Greek

🍶 *5 oz*

This recipe is perfect for pairing with a fresh farmer's market Greek salad or for Greekifying grilled fish.

2 tablespoons of red wine vinegar

1/2 teaspoon of sea salt

1/8 teaspoon of freshly ground black pepper

1/2 teaspoon of dried oregano

4 tablespoons of olive oil

4 tablespoons of canola oil

i. Combine vinegar, salt, and pepper in an 8 oz Mason jar.

ii. Seal and shake for 30 seconds.

iii. Add oregano and oils, seal, and shake for 30 seconds more.

The Spaniard

🍶 *5 oz*

This dressing adds a Spanish twist to salads. We like to use it with a salad of spicy arugula, charred red peppers, and manchego cheese.

2 tablespoons of sherry vinegar

1/2 teaspoon of chopped anchovies

1/4 teaspoon of sea salt

1/8 teaspoon of freshly ground black pepper

1/2 clove of fresh garlic, cut in half lengthwise

4 tablespoons of olive oil

4 tablespoons of canola oil

i. Combine vinegar, anchovies, salt, and pepper in an 8 oz Mason jar.

ii. Seal and shake for 30 seconds.

iii. Add garlic and oils, seal, and shake for 30 seconds more.

Snap Pea & Herb Salad
with The Essential Vinaigrette

A verdant combination of crisp snap peas and pungent green herbs, topped with salty Pecorino Romano cheese.

✖ *Serves 4*

3 cups of snap peas, strings removed

1 cup of mixed green herbs, washed and large stems removed (we love flat leaf parsley, mint, and dill)

5 oz of The Essential Vinaigrette (page 32)

1 pinch of sea salt

1 pinch of freshly ground black pepper

1/2 cup of finely shaved Pecorino Romano cheese

i.   Add snap peas and herbs to a large bowl.

ii. Toss with The Essential Vinaigrette, salt, and pepper until evenly distributed.

iii. Top with shaved Pecorino Romano cheese and garnish with a few leftover mixed herbs.

Kale & Apple Salad
with The Orchard Vinaigrette

Hearty with kale and apples and spiked with blue cheese and toasted walnuts, this is our go-to cool-weather salad.

✖ *Serves 4*

3 apples (we like Stayman or Honeycrisp varieties)

1 bunch of Tuscan kale, center stems removed

1/2 cup of toasted walnuts

5 oz of The Orchard Vinaigrette (page 32)

1 pinch of sea salt

1 pinch of freshly ground black pepper

1/2 cup of crumbled blue cheese

i.   Slice the apples into 1/8-inch slices. Tear the kale into pieces and combine with the apple slices in a large bowl.

ii. Add the walnuts and toss with The Orchard Vinaigrette, salt, and pepper until evenly distributed.

iii. Top with blue cheese.

Sea Salt

Garlic

Black Pepper

Olive Oil

Thyme

Garlic is slowly roasted with thyme and black pepper in this savory garlic confit oil

1 head of garlic

Sea salt

Freshly ground black pepper

1 cup of extra virgin olive oil

5 whole black peppercorns

4 sprigs of fresh thyme

---

i.   Preheat the oven to 300 degrees. Rinse the head of garlic and cut off the top, exposing the cloves. Season the exposed edges with salt and pepper and place facedown in a deep baking dish.

ii.   Add the olive oil, peppercorns, and fresh thyme to the baking dish, cover with aluminum foil, and roast for one hour.

iii.   Remove from the oven and let cool for 30 minutes, covered.

iv.   Uncover and remove the garlic, placing on a towel to drain. Strain the oil through cheesecloth and into an 8 oz Mason jar, adding one fresh sprig of thyme.

v.   Squeeze the cloves of garlic from the head and add them to the Mason jar. The infusion and roasted garlic cloves will keep in the refrigerator for up to one month.

Great for adding even more flavor to Seared Feather Steak (turn to page 61 for the recipe), for serving with grilled bread, and for elevating simple roasted potatoes.

---

umami alert!

Don't let the roasted garlic cloves in this infusion go to waste! Use them alongside the infused oil. They have a caramelized, umami-packed richness you won't want to miss.

Garlic
Confit Oil
with
thyme and black pepper

⏰ 2 hours   🥛 8 oz

Infused with deliciously fragrant roasted garlic, this olive oil infusion serves as the backbone for much of what we cook.

Fish Sauce

Thai Chilies

spicy chilies and savory fish sauce make up the signature condiment of Thailand: Prik Nam Pla

Prik Nam Pla

⏱ *Immediate* 🫙 *4 oz*

4 fresh Thai chilies (green or red)

4 oz of fish sauce

---

i.   Thinly slice the chilies into rounds.

ii.   Combine with the fish sauce in an 8 oz Mason jar.

iii. Seal and shake for 5 seconds.

iv.   Use immediately as you would hot sauce, spooning out the chilies if you crave extra heat. Keeps for up to three days in the refrigerator (but we tend to make it fresh each time).

Great for upping the heat level of your favorite takeout Thai dishes like curry with sticky rice, noodle dishes, and fried rice.

---

a kitchen essential

Used like salt and pepper, fish sauce is a staple seasoning in southeast Asian cooking. Don't be intimidated by its pungent aroma. Small doses add a uniquely savory element to food.

This isn't *technically* an oil, but this spicy Thai infusion combines fish sauce and Thai chilies to create a condiment that can be found on every table in Thailand, and we absolutely love it. We've been known to add it to just about anything that needs a kick of savory heat.

flash-
infused
oils

Restaurants have been using herb-infused oils to deepen the flavor of finished dishes for a long time, but up until now those oils have rarely made an appearance in the home. We have created a quick-and-easy method for making flash-infused oils with basic infusing tools, but be sure to use the freshest herbs you can find; the better the herbs, the tastier the finished infusion will be. We like to use a blend of a flavorful oil (such as extra virgin olive oil or walnut oil) and a flavorless oil (such as canola oil) in these infusions so the flavors of the oils complement, rather than overpower, the delicious herbs.

Step 1:
muddle

To start an herb infusion, add coarse sea salt and fresh herbs to an 8 oz Mason jar and muddle the ingredients until the herbs are thoroughly crushed. The large grains of sea salt help to break down the fresh herbs and release more flavor into the infusion.

Next, add the oil, seal the Mason jar, and shake for 30 seconds. By shaking the jar, you accelerate the transfer of flavors from the herbs to the oils and get the most flavor out of the ingredients.

Step 2:

shake

strain

For the final step, strain the infused oil through cheesecloth to remove the flecks of herbs and clarify the oil, squeezing the crushed herbs to extract as much flavor as possible. The finished oil will keep in the refrigerator for up to three days.

Basil Oil

6 oz

This oil is great for adding an extra layer of basil goodness to a Burrata Caprese Salad (turn the page for the recipe).

1 cup (packed) of fresh basil

1/2 teaspoon of coarse sea salt

6 tablespoons of olive oil

6 tablespoons of canola oil

i. Combine basil and salt in an 8 oz Mason jar and muddle until thoroughly crushed and aromatic.

ii. Add oils, seal, and shake for 30 seconds.

iii. Strain through cheesecloth, squeezing the crushed basil to extract all the oil.

Rosemary-Mint Oil

6 oz

We like to use this infusion for putting the finishing touch on steak tartare and seasoning grilled lamb chops.

3 sprigs of fresh rosemary

3 sprigs of fresh mint

1/2 teaspoon of coarse sea salt

6 tablespoons of olive oil

6 tablespoons of canola oil

i. Combine the herbs and salt in an 8 oz Mason jar and muddle until thoroughly crushed and aromatic.

ii. Add oils, seal, and shake for 30 seconds.

iii. Strain through cheesecloth, squeezing the crushed herbs to extract all the oil.

Sage Oil

6 oz

Nothing tops off a warm fall butternut squash soup or roasted sweet potatoes like this nutty, herbaceous infused oil.

1/2 cup (packed) of fresh sage

1/2 teaspoon of coarse sea salt

6 tablespoons of walnut oil

6 tablespoons of canola oil

i. Combine the sage and salt in an 8 oz Mason jar and muddle until thoroughly crushed and aromatic.

ii. Add oils, seal, and shake for 30 seconds.

iii. Strain through cheesecloth, squeezing the crushed sage to extract all the oil.

2 large heirloom tomatoes

1 cup of mixed cherry tomatoes

8 oz burrata cheese

Sea salt

Freshly ground black pepper

Basil Oil (page 49)

1 bunch of basil leaves

---

i. Slice the heirloom tomatoes into 1/2 inch rounds and arrange in a layer on a plate. Halve the cherry tomatoes and arrange on top of the base layer.

ii. Place the burrata in the middle of the plate on top of the tomatoes. Add salt and pepper to taste and drizzle Basil Oil over the tomatoes.

iii. Finish with leaves of basil and an extra dose of Basil Oil. Serve with good crusty bread.

Burrata Caprese Salad
with basil oil

 Serves 4

Featuring a mix of sliced heirloom tomatoes, creamy burrata, and basil and finished with our Basil Oil, this is our take on the classic Italian caprese salad. Hello, summer. You rock.

Popcorn
Kernels

Honey

SRIRACHA HOT CHILI SAUCE
TƯƠNG ỚT SRIRACHA
匯豐食品公司
HUY FONG FOODS, INC.
4800 Azusa Canyon Rd., Irwindale, CA 91706
(626) 286-8328
ww..e.huyfong.com
NET WT. 28 OZ. (1 lb. 12 oz.)(793g)(740mL)

Sriracha

Butter

worth it.

skip the prepackaged stuff and pop real kernels for this sweet and spicy popcorn

4 tablespoons of butter

1 tablespoon of honey

1 teaspoon of sriracha hot sauce

1/4 cup of popcorn kernels

2 tablespoons of canola oil

Sea salt

---

i.   Place the butter and honey in an 8 oz Mason jar and microwave, uncovered, for 30 seconds.

ii.   Add the sriracha and stir to combine.

iii.   Combine the popcorn kernels and canola oil in a heavy bottomed pan and cook on the stove, covered, over medium-high heat, shaking occasionally. Remove from heat once the popping stops.

iv.   Place in a bowl and top with the infused butter. Sprinkle with sea salt and enjoy.

Movie Night

with fresh popcorn

✕ *Serves 2*

A quick-and-easy way to amp up your next movie night? A sweet and spicy infused butter to top fresh homemade popcorn.

rooftop Italian

There are few better things than an alfresco dinner shared with great friends. Since backyards are hard to come by in our Brooklyn neighborhood, we head to the roof to grill up an Italian-inspired meal for our crew. There's grilled pizza bianca with spicy chili oil, caprese salad with basil oil, and steak with charred lemon and garlic confit oil. Oh, and some fresh limoncello we made the night before. Soak it all in—it's the best time of year.

Grilled Pizza Bianca
with Olio Santo
Page 26

Burrata Caprese Salad
with Basil Oil
Page 51

58

2 feather steaks (or your favorite cut), approx. 1 lb each

4 tablespoons Garlic Confit Oil (plus more for finishing, see page 39)

Sea salt

Freshly ground black pepper

1 lemon, cut in half

---

i.   Preheat a grill at high direct heat.

ii.   Rub the steaks with 4 tablespoons of Garlic Confit Oil and season liberally with salt and pepper. Oil and season the cut edges of the lemon.

iii. Grill the steak to medium-rare (approximately 4–5 minutes per side). Meanwhile, add the lemon halves facedown on high heat alongside the steak and cook until charred.

iv.   Let the steak rest for 5 minutes, then slice. Finish with a drizzle of Garlic Confit Oil, and serve with charred lemon.

Seared Feather Steak

with garlic confit oil

✗ *Serves 4*

Sometimes called a ribeye cap, the feather steak is the greatest steak you've probably never heard of. Feather steak is the beautifully marbled and tender outside layer of the more common ribeye steak, and is our favorite cut of beef. We like to finish off ours with a drizzle of Garlic Confit Oil and a squeeze of charred lemon to cut the richness.

Overnight
Limoncello
Page 89

spirit

Infusing spirits is just plain fun. The potential combinations of ingredients and base spirits are nearly endless, and the fast-infusing properties of alcohol allow you to create flavorful infusions quickly. In this section you'll find a collection of our favorite recipes and techniques for infusing spirits, including everything from smoky infused mezcal (page 75) to a method for making your own fruit-infused spirits in a flash (page 96). Infused spirits are best enjoyed with friends, like at a long Sunday brunch (page 118).

Summer Peaches

Kentucky Bourbon

every summer we take a trip to the farmer's market
to pick up crates of peak-season peaches to make
peach-infused bourbon

Summer   Peaches

2 fresh peaches, peeled, pitted, and cut into eighths

14 oz of Kentucky bourbon

---

i. Place the peaches in a 16 oz Mason jar and add the bourbon. Seal and shake just to combine.

ii. Let sit in a cool, dark place for four weeks to allow the bourbon to infuse.

iii. Strain the infused bourbon through cheesecloth, squeezing out excess liquid from the peaches. The infusion will keep for up to one year stored in a cool, dark place.

Great for bourbon cocktails. Turn the page for the recipe for The Spiced Peach Bourbon Old Fashioned or head to page 123 for our version of a hot toddy to keep you warm on a dark winter night.

---

patience is a virtue

Some things really do get better with age. This infusion is one of them. With time it gets sweeter, juicier, and more delicious. Just you wait.

Peach Bourbon

the best part of summer's end

🕐 4 weeks   🥃 14 oz

We first started making peach bourbon in college. Peach season in southern Virginia ends with a dramatic rush of ripe fruit right during the final days of summer. To preserve that fleeting flavor, we would pick up crates of peaches on the cheap and add them to bourbon. The result? An infused bourbon that will remind you of summer all year.

peachy.

the Spiced Peach Bourbon Old Fashioned

X *Makes one cocktail*

1 cube of cane sugar

5 dashes of aromatic bitters

3 oz of Peach Bourbon (page 69)

2 cloves

1 stick of cinnamon (plus 1 to garnish)

1 slice of fresh peach (to garnish)

i. Add the cane sugar cubes and bitters to a cocktail mixing glass.

ii. Muddle the ingredients in the bottom of the mixing glass until the sugar has mostly dissolved. Add the Peach Bourbon and spices.

iii. Add ice to above the level of the liquid and stir for 15 seconds. Strain the mixture into a rocks glass containing a single large cube of ice.

iv. Garnish with the remaining cinnamon and peach slice.

Mezcal

Roasted Pineapple

Roasted   Pineapple

roasting fruit brings out rich, caramelized flavors,
which transfer beautifully to this pineapple-infused mezcal

Roasted Pineapple Mezcal

⏱ 48 hours   🥃 12 oz

A bold spirit like mezcal (basically a smoky tequila) makes for a potent yet delicious infusion. The richly caramelized, tropical flavors of roasted pineapple smooth out the sharp edges of the mezcal to create something truly special and utterly delicious.

12 one-inch cubes of fresh pineapple, peel removed

12 oz of mezcal

___

i. Preheat the oven to 375 degrees. Place the pineapple on an unlined nonstick baking sheet and roast for one hour (or until slightly browned). Let cool.

ii. Combine the pineapple and mezcal in a 16 oz Mason jar, seal, and shake for 30 seconds.

iii. Let sit at room temperature for 48 hours.

iv. Strain through cheesecloth, squeezing out any excess liquid.

v. Use in cocktails or simply served over ice. The infusion will keep in the refrigerator for up to three months.

Great for putting a new spin on the classic margarita or sipping neat, chased with an ice-cold Mexican beer.

___

add some smoke

Mezcal is tequila's more exciting cousin. Like tequila, it is distilled from the agave plant, but a unique underground roasting process gives mezcal its deliciously smoky taste.

Cocoa

Cream

Espresso

Condensed Milk

Irish Whiskey

Vanilla Bean

using real vanilla bean in this Irish Cream sets the finished
infusion apart from the store-bought variety

4 oz of sweetened condensed milk

4 oz of heavy cream

Seeds from 1 vanilla bean

1 teaspoon of unsweetened cocoa powder

5 oz of Irish whiskey

1 & 1/2 oz of espresso, chilled

---

i. Combine the condensed milk, cream, vanilla bean, and cocoa powder in a 16 oz Mason jar.

ii. Stir briefly, seal, and shake until combined and the cocoa powder has dissolved.

iii. Working quickly to avoid curdling, add the whiskey and espresso, seal again, and shake for 20 seconds to combine. The Irish Cream will keep in the refrigerator for up to two weeks.

Great for adding a bit of punch to your after-dinner coffee; keep this on hand during the long holiday season.

---

act fast

It's important to shake the Mason jar vigorously when you add the whiskey to the milk and cream to avoid curdling.

Irish Cream

🕐 *Immediate*   🥃 *16 oz*

This homemade Irish Cream is light-years better than that stale bottle you'll find at your local liquor store. The decadent combination of good Irish whiskey, cream, and real vanilla bean makes for a smooth and sippable liqueur.

Be sure to use a decent-quality Irish whiskey for this recipe; the smoother the flavors of the whiskey are, the better your Irish Cream will be.

Hot Sauce

Horseradish

Pickle Brine

Crab
Seasoning

Black Pepper

Garlic

Vodka

Dill

Pickle Brine

spicy pickle brine is the not-so-secret ingredient
in our Bloody Mary concentrate

6 oz of vodka

6 oz of pickle brine

4 sprigs of fresh dill

1 clove of garlic, halved

10 black peppercorns

2 teaspoons of crab seasoning (such as Old Bay)

2 teaspoons of horseradish, freshly grated (if available)

1 teaspoon of hot sauce

---

i.   Combine all ingredients in a 16 oz Mason jar. Seal and shake until combined and the seasoning has dissolved.

ii.   Infuse in the refrigerator for 12 hours.

iii.   Strain through cheesecloth. The infusion will keep in the refrigerator for up to two weeks.

Ready to mix up a Bloody Mary in an instant? Turn the page for our recipe for the Best Bloody Mary.

---

the secret's out

The not-so-secret key ingredient to the best Bloody Mary recipes? Pickle brine. After finishing off a jar of pickles, be sure to save the brine. It'll come in handy when Bloody Mary time rolls around.

the
Bloody
Anytime

🕐 *12 hours.*   🥛 *14 oz*

It's hard to imagine weekend brunch without the classic Bloody Mary, but most bottled mixes just don't cut it. So we like to infuse our own Bloody Mary concentrate to have on hand anytime. Sunday Funday will never be the same again.

we like to garnish our Bloody Mary with fresh herbs and an assortment of pickles

Garnishes

the Best Bloody Mary

✕ *Makes one cocktail*

3 oz of The Bloody Anytime (page 83)

4 oz of tomato juice

Garnishes (we use fresh parsley, dill, and celery leaves, along with pickled green beans and caper berries)

i. Combine The Bloody Anytime with tomato juice in a cocktail shaker.

ii. Shake for 5 seconds to combine and strain into a glass filled with ice.

iii. Finish with your favorite garnishes.

Vodka

Lemons

Simple Syrup

using whole slices of fresh lemon speeds up the
infusing process for this quick Limoncello

5 oz of vodka

5 oz of simple syrup (see below for recipe)

1 lemon, sliced into rounds approximately 1/4 inch thick

---

i.   Combine all ingredients in a 16 oz Mason jar. Seal and shake until combined.

ii.   Let infuse at room temperature for 12 hours.

iii.   Strain through cheesecloth. The infusion will keep in the refrigerator for up to three months.

To make the simple syrup: Combine 1/2 cup of sugar and 1/2 cup of water in a saucepan over low heat until the sugar is dissolved. Let cool before using.

---

bitter is better

While it may seem natural to remove the pith, the white layer between the lemon and the peel, we prefer to leave it on. The pith adds a slight bitter note to the infusion, which we love.

Overnight
Limoncello

⏰ *12 hours*   🥤 *10 oz*

Popular along Italy's Amalfi coast where lemon trees grow in abundance, Limoncello is a citrusy after-dinner liqueur. Most recipes for the fragrant drink take weeks to execute. That's why we developed the Overnight Limoncello, a super-fast method to craft a tasty Limoncello-inspired liqueur in just 12 hours. By using a large number of sliced lemon rounds, we increase the surface area of flavorful citrus, speeding up the infusion process.

Jalapeños

Gin

Cucumbers

piquant chilies and cooling cucumbers meet
in this spicy cucumber gin

Spicy
Cucumber
Gin

⏰ *12 hours* 🥛 *12 oz*

A tasty blend of spicy jalapeños, cooling cucumber, and herbaceous gin makes for a delicious infused spirit you can use in a variety of cocktails.

12 oz of gin

10 sliced rounds of cucumber

1/2 of a jalapeño, halved lengthwise and seeds removed

---

i. Combine all ingredients in a 16 oz Mason jar. Seal and shake for three seconds.

ii. Let infuse at room temperature for 12 hours.

iii. Strain through cheesecloth. The infusion will keep in the refrigerator for up to two weeks.

Great for spicing up your standard gin & tonic or putting a new twist on a classic cocktail (turn the page for The Spicy Cucumber Gimlet).

---

some like it hot

The longer this infusion sits, the spicier it gets. So be sure to taste the jalapeño before using. If it's especially spicy, simply remove the pepper early on in the infusing process.

the Spicy Cucumber Gimlet

🥃 *Makes one cocktail*

This is a spicy, savory take on the classic gin cocktail, the gimlet. Traditionally a shaken cocktail made with dry gin and sweetened lime juice, this version subsitutes in Spicy Cucumber Gin, fresh lime juice, and simple syrup for a delicious result.

2 & 1/4 oz of Spicy Cucumber Gin (page 93)

3/4 oz of lime juice

3/4 oz of simple syrup (see below for recipe)

1 sliced round of cucumber

---

i.   Combine the Spicy Cucumber Gin, lime juice, and simple syrup in a cocktail shaker.

ii.   Add ice to above the liquid and shake for 15 seconds.

iii.   Strain into a chilled coupe glass and garnish with a round of cucumber.

To make the simple syrup: Combine 1/2 cup of sugar and 1/2 cup of water in a saucepan over low heat until the sugar is dissolved. Let cool before using.

spicy.
tart.
sweet.

fresh
fruit-
infused
spirits

Eschew those artificially flavored fruity spirits that you find on your liquor store's shelf for the fresh, bright taste of homemade fruit-infused spirits. These flash infusions are so quick and easy to prepare that you'll never touch the store-bought stuff again. We guarantee it.

the method

It's easy to master the technique for making a fresh fruit-infused spirit. Just add ripe fruit to a Mason jar, muddle to release the flavors of the fruit, and pour in your spirit. After a quick shake, strain the infusion through cheesecloth to remove any pieces of fruit and you're done.

When you're deciding what to make, think about which fruits are in season and pick from those options. We've chosen four of our favorite fruit-spirit pairings, but the possibilities for combinations are limited only by your imagination—and rate of consumption.

Grapefruit Tequila   Cranberry Rum   Blueberry Vodka   Cherry Bourbon

Fresh Cranberries

Grapefruit Tequila
🥃 *14 oz*

Great for whipping up margaritas, substituting Grapefruit Tequila for the regular tequila in your favorite recipe.

10 strips of grapefruit zest (white pith removed)

1 cube of cane sugar

14 oz of tequila

i. Place grapefruit zest and cane sugar in a 16 oz Mason jar and muddle until fragrant.

ii. Add tequila, seal, and shake for 30 seconds.

iii. Strain through cheesecloth, squeezing to extract excess liquid. Infusion will keep in the refrigerator for up to one month.

Cranberry Rum
🥃 *14 oz*

Great for making a Cranberry Rum Punch (turn the page for the recipe) or for spiking sparkling apple cider.

1/2 cup of fresh cranberries

14 oz of white rum

i. Place cranberries in a 16 oz Mason jar and muddle until crushed.

ii. Add rum, seal, and shake for 30 seconds.

iii. Strain through cheesecloth, squeezing to extract excess liquid. Infusion will keep in the refrigerator for up to one month.

Blueberry Vodka 🥃 *14 oz*

Great for serving on the rocks with a splash of club soda and lime.

1/2 cup of fresh blueberries

14 oz of vodka

i. Place blueberries in a 16 oz Mason jar and muddle until crushed.

ii. Add vodka, seal, and shake for 30 seconds.

iii. Strain through cheesecloth, squeezing to extract excess liquid. Infusion will keep in the refrigerator for up to one month.

Cherry Bourbon 🥃 *14 oz*

Great for adding a new spin to traditional bourbon-based cocktails like the Old Fashioned or Manhattan.

10 fresh cherries, pits removed

14 oz of bourbon

i. Place cherries in a 16 oz Mason jar and muddle until thoroughly crushed.

ii. Add bourbon, seal, and shake for 30 seconds.

iii. Strain through cheesecloth, squeezing to extract excess liquid. Infusion will keep in the refrigerator for up to one month.

Cranberry Rum Punch

X *Makes one cocktail*

3/4 oz of fresh lime juice

3 cubes of cane sugar

1 & 1/2 oz of Cranberry Rum (page 100)

3 dashes of aromatic bitters

1 pinch of ground cloves

1 pinch of ground cinnamon

Sparkling wine

2 cranberries

1 stick of cinnamon

This rum punch was inspired by the classic holiday flavors of fresh cranberries and warm mulling spices, and uses ingredients that many people have in their homes during the holiday season (no need to add to your shopping list). The punch is also easy to make in large batches, making it perfect for entertaining a crowd. Just shake up 3 or 4 at a time in a cocktail shaker, pour into glasses, and top with sparkling wine.

i. Add the lime juice and cane sugar to a cocktail shaker and muddle the ingredients until the sugar is mostly dissolved.

ii. Add the Cranberry Rum, bitters, cloves, and cinnamon. Add ice to above the liquid, seal, and shake for 10 seconds.

iii. Strain into rocks glass filled with ice. Top with sparkling wine and garnish with cranberries and a stick of cinnamon.

spiced.

Turbinado
Simple Syrup

Cloves

Star Anise

Cinnamon

Pear Brandy

Pears

star anise adds a striking flavor and a celebratory visual to this fall liqueur, ushering in the holiday season

Star Anise

7 oz of pear brandy or eau de vie (or substitute in your favorite vodka)

3 oz of turbinado simple syrup (see below for recipe)

1 ripe pear, peeled and sliced into eighths

1 stick of cinnamon

1 small star anise pod

2 cloves

---

i. Combine all ingredients in a 16 oz Mason jar. Seal and shake for 30 seconds.

ii. Let infuse at room temperature for 24 hours.

iii. Strain through cheesecloth, squeezing to extract excess liquid.

iv. Chill before serving. The infusion will keep in the refrigerator for up to three months.

To make the turbinado simple syrup: Combine 1/2 cup of turbinado sugar and 1/2 cup of water in a saucepan over low heat until the sugar is dissolved. Let cool before using.

Spiced
Pear Liqueur
with warm fall spices

⏲ *24 hours*   🥃 *10 oz*

Each fall, we make sure to pick up pears at the peak of their season and combine them with pear brandy and holiday spices to create an after-dinner liqueur that we can enjoy through the end of the year.

Vanilla Bean

Turbinado
Simple Syrup

Aged Rum

Coffee

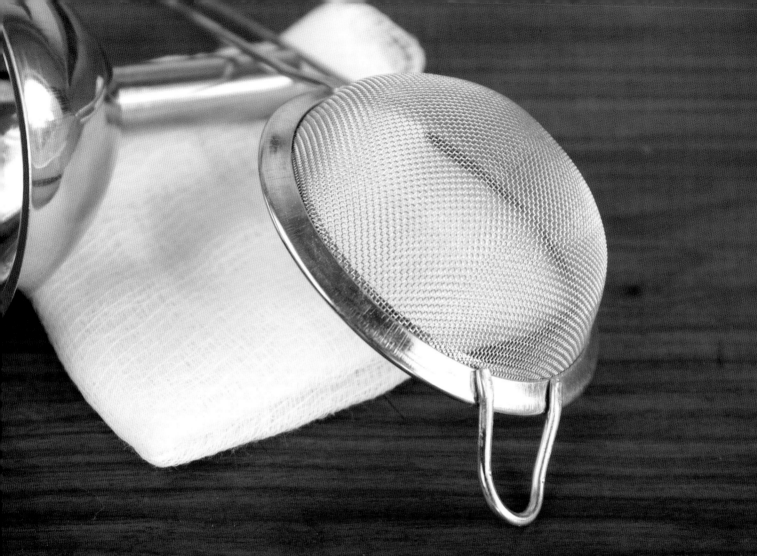

this coffee liqueur requires a double straining process
to avoid grit in the finished infusion

8 oz of aged rum

4 oz of turbinado simple syrup (see below for recipe)

1/2 cup of whole bean coffee, coarsely ground

Seeds from 1/2 of a vanilla bean

---

i.   Combine all ingredients in a 16 oz Mason jar. Seal and shake to combine. Refrigerate and let infuse for 24 hours.

ii. Strain through a double layer of cheesecloth. The infusion will keep in the refrigerator for up to three months.

To make the turbinado simple syrup: Combine 1/2 cup of turbinado sugar and 1/2 cup of water in a saucepan over low heat until the sugar is dissolved. Let cool before using.

---

quality matters

When rum shopping, be sure to pick out a high-quality bottle that you would be okay drinking on its own. Look for rum that has been aged for at least five years. The rich caramelization from a well-aged rum lends a wonderful depth of flavor to this liqueur.

Coffee
Liqueur

⏰ *24 hours*   🥛 *12 oz*

Though coffee liqueurs line liquor store shelves, they tend to be overly sugary and altogether not delicious. The remedy? Make your own! It's a surprisingly simple process that will make you wonder why you ever bought the commercial stuff to begin with. This rum-based coffee liqueur is great in cocktails or doused over vanilla ice cream for an impromptu dessert.

the homemade White Russian

Channel the Dude and make yourself a completely homemade version of the classic White Russian Cocktail, using Coffee Liqueur and half-and-half.

2 oz of vodka

1 oz of Coffee Liqueur (page 111)

1 oz of half-and-half

---

i. Add the vodka and Coffee Liqueur to a rocks glass filled with ice.

ii. Top with half-and-half and stir to combine.

classic.

Whiskey

Cinnamon

Turbinado
Simple Syrup

we use spicy whole cinnamon sticks to flavor
this fiery infused whiskey

10 oz of whiskey

6 oz of turbinado simple syrup (see below for recipe)

4 sticks of cinnamon

---

i. Combine all ingredients in a 16 oz Mason jar. Seal and shake to combine.

ii. Let infuse at room temperature for 24 hours.

iii. Strain through cheesecloth and chill in the freezer before serving.

iv. The infusion will keep in the refrigerator for up to three months.

To make the turbinado simple syrup: Combine 1/2 cup of turbinado sugar and 1/2 cup of water in a saucepan over low heat until the sugar is dissolved. Let cool before using.

---

want it spicier?

If you're like us and can't get enough spicy cinnamon heat, just up the amount of cinnamon in this recipe. You won't regret it.

⏰ 24 hours   🥃 16 oz

The now-ubiquitous, buy-the-bar-a-round shot with a name that rhymes with "birefall" gets the upgrade it needs. Whiskey, turbinado simple syrup, and real cinnamon sticks infuse together to create a spicy cinnamon-infused whiskey that you will be proud to pour into your friends' shot glasses.

sunday brunch

118

When the vicious New York winter sets in, the only antidote to the cold is a soul-warming Sunday brunch with friends. Our fail-safe recipe to cure the Polar Vortex blues: whole wheat blueberry pancakes, freshly squeezed mimosas, and "hot tea-dies" spiked with peach-infused bourbon. Come on in, drink up, and pretend tomorrow's not Monday...

Peach Bourbon Hot Tea-dy

with earl grey tea

✕ *Makes two cocktails*

Sweetened with honey and spiked with Peach Bourbon, this version of a hot toddy carries with it sun-drenched flavors of summer for warmth in the dead of winter. Or maybe that's just the whiskey talking.

1 & 1/2 oz of Peach Bourbon (page 69)

3/4 oz of lemon juice

3 tablespoons of honey

2 bags of Earl Grey tea

Boiling water

2 strips of lemon zest (to garnish)

i.   Add the Peach Bourbon, lemon juice, honey, and tea bags to a 32 oz Mason jar.

ii.   Add boiling water to fill 1/3 of the jar (approximately 10 oz), stir to combine, and let steep for two minutes.

iii. Strain mixture into teacups and garnish with lemon zest.

warm up.

Whole Wheat **Blueberry Pancakes**

with Blueberry-Infused Maple Syrup

✗ *Serves 2*

These pancakes are the MVP of Sunday brunch. We use a blend of whole wheat and white flours in this recipe to give the pancakes a hearty flavor, while still keeping the texture light and airy. A quick-infused blueberry maple syrup finishes the dish and makes these pancakes feel extra special. We wouldn't blame you if you added a bit of whipped cream...it's still the weekend, right?

For the pancakes:

3/4 cup of all-purpose flour

3/4 cup of whole wheat flour

3 tablespoons of sugar

1 & 3/4 teaspoons of baking powder

1 teaspoon of salt

1 & 1/2 cups of milk

3 tablespoons of butter, melted

1 teaspoon vanilla extract

2 eggs, whites and yolks separated, whites beaten until stiff peaks form

1 cup of fresh blueberries

For the infused syrup:

10 tablespoons of maple syrup

1/2 cup of fresh blueberries

To make the pancakes:

i. Combine all dry ingredients in a large bowl. In a separate bowl, add the milk, butter, vanilla, and egg yolks and whisk until blended.

ii. Add the wet ingredients to the dry ingredients and whisk quickly until just combined, being careful not to overbeat. Fold in the egg whites.

iii. Preheat a nonstick pan over medium heat. Add 1/4 cup of batter per pancake to the pan, adding 4-5 blueberries to each pancake. Cook for 2-3 minutes, or until bubbles have appeared. Flip the pancakes and cook for 2-3 more minutes.

iv. Remove the pancakes and serve at once with the blueberry-infused maple syrup.

To make the infused syrup:

Add the maple syrup and blueberries to a bowl and microwave uncovered for 30 seconds, or until the blueberries begin to burst. Serve warm.

water

Water is the most versatile, blank-canvas liquid for infusing. Our variety of water infusions includes an invigoratingly healthy hangover cure (page 135), cold-brewed iced teas infused with fresh fruit (page 148), and a salted lime syrup (page 161) that can be used to mix up craft cocktails, which, in turn, elevate a casual weeknight delivery meal of Thai food at home (page 162). We'll drink to that.

Cucumber

Lime

Water

Mint

cucumbers and mint have a cooling
effect during hot summer months

Cucumber Mint Water

⏰ *Immediate* 🥛 *32 oz*

As much as we love the hot days of summer, it's sometimes hard to escape that sticky feeling. Enter this cooling infusion. Lime, cucumber, and mint work together to create a refreshing sip that we keep in the fridge all summer long.

12 slices of cucumber

4 slices of lime

4 large sprigs of fresh mint

28 oz of water

i. Combine the cucumber, lime, and mint in a 32 oz Mason jar. Muddle until lightly crushed.

ii. Add the water, seal, and shake for 30 seconds to combine.

iii. Serve over ice. The infusion will keep in the refrigerator for up to 24 hours.

Great for cooling down on hot summer days and feeling like you are drinking your vegetables (in a good way).

what kind of water?

For all our water infusions we suggest using filtered tap water or bottled spring water for the freshest-tasting infusions. Don't have either? Tap water can work, in a pinch.

refreshing.

Cayenne Pepper

Turmeric

Agave

Lemon

Water

Ginger

ground turmeric, the key ingredient in this hangover cure,
is a powerful antioxidant that helps your body detox

12 slices of fresh ginger, peeled

26 oz of water

3 oz of fresh lemon juice

3 oz of agave syrup

1/2 teaspoon of ground turmeric

2 large pinches of ground cayenne pepper

---

i.   Add the ginger slices to a 32 oz Mason jar and muddle until thoroughly crushed.

ii.   Add the remaining ingredients to the jar, seal, and shake for 30 seconds to combine.

iii. Strain through cheesecloth and serve over ice. The infusion will keep in the refrigerator for up to two days.

Great for combating pesky hangovers and curing cases of general Sunday morning laziness.

---

did you know?

Ginger and turmeric make a powerful team when it comes to fighting hangovers. Ginger naturally calms your stomach while turmeric works to detoxify the liver. A glass or two of this infusion is just what you need to get back up and running on Sunday morning.

The
Sunday Morning
Reviver

⏱ *Immediate* 🥛 *32 oz*

Spicy fresh ginger, tart lemon, and cayenne pepper pair up with healthful turmeric in this cleansing and refreshing infusion. We like to mix this up on weekend mornings when a detox from the night before is very much in order.

135

Coffee

Water

Condensed Milk

when making this overnight cold brew, be sure to coarsely grind your beans to avoid unwanted sediment

Ground   Coffee

28 oz of water

1 cup of whole bean coffee, coarsely ground

Sweetened condensed milk

---

i.   Combine the water and ground coffee in a 32 oz Mason jar. Seal
        and shake to combine.

ii.   Refrigerate for 14 hours.

iii.   Strain the coffee through a double layer of cheesecloth.

iv.   Serve over ice and top with sweetened condensed milk. The cold
        brew coffee will keep in the refrigerator for up to three days.

---

don't like it sweet?

If you don't like your iced coffee sweet, just omit the condensed milk in
the final step. The cold brew recipe produces some fine coffee that can
be enjoyed all by itself.

The
Hanoi
Cold Brew

🕐 *14 hours*   🥛 *28 oz*

In our Brooklyn workshop, we've been known to go through iced coffee at an alarmingly high speed. But when we're looking for something a little different, we take inspiration from Vietnam, where iced coffee and sweetened condensed milk come together to create something special. The condensed milk adds a richness to the deeply flavorful cold-brewed coffee, setting this recipe apart from your standard iced coffee.

Agave

Jalapeños

Water

Grapefruit

we like to mellow out the heat of the
jalapeños in this infused grapefruit water
by removing the seeds

Extra Spicy

🕐 *Immediate*   🥛 *32 oz*

Grapefruit and jalapeños are a match made in infusion heaven. The tartness of the grapefruit juice is naturally balanced out by sweet agave and a hint of heat from fresh jalapeños. Tequila optional (but really, when is tequila ever not an option?).

20 oz of water

10 oz of freshly squeezed grapefruit juice

1 oz of raw agave

3 slices of jalapeño chili pepper, seeds removed

---

i.   Combine all ingredients in a 32 oz Mason jar.

ii.   Seal and shake to combine for 30 seconds.

iii.   Serve over ice. The infusion will keep in the refrigerator for up to 24 hours.

---

hot hot heat

Taste the jalapeño before using it in this infusion to gauge spice levels. Some peppers pack more of a punch than others, so you may need to adjust the recipe to better accommodate for your preferred spice level.

Sherry Vinegar

Honey

Ginger

Water

sherry vinegar adds a tangy Spanish accent to this old-school American thirst-quencher

20 slices of fresh ginger, peeled

30 oz of water

2 oz of sherry vinegar

2.5 oz of honey

---

i.   Add the ginger slices to a 32 oz Mason jar and muddle until thoroughly crushed.

ii.   Add the water, sherry vinegar, and honey, seal, and shake to combine.

iii.   Refrigerate for 12 hours.

iv.   Strain through cheesecloth, squeezing excess liquid from the ginger.

v.   Serve over ice. The infusion will keep in the refrigerator for up to three days.

Great for impressing your hipster friends. Sure, they've heard of shrubs, but have they heard of switchel?

---

mix it up

Switchel tastes great on its own, but it's also a delicious cocktail ingredient. Try mixing 4 oz of switchel with 1 oz of whiskey or dark rum for a super quick and tasty drink.

Spanish Switchel

with sherry vinegar

🕐 *12 hours*   🥛 *32 oz*

Made by infusing water and vinegar with fresh ginger, the switchel dates back to colonial times when farmers drank the bracing beverage to quench their thirst during the hay harvest. Fast forward to present day, where we've updated the old recipe by adding sherry vinegar and honey to the mix.

cold-
brewed
teas

Southerners take iced tea seriously. Where we're from it's customary to keep a pitcher of ice-cold tea ready for visitors. Inspired by this tradition, we have upgraded the traditional hot-brewed iced tea by using a cold-brewing technique combined with fresh flavoring ingredients. Cold brewing tea for several hours slowly draws out the core flavors of the tea without unwanted bitter and astringent notes, and it actually reduces the amount of caffeine in the finished tea. The addition of fruit and herbs during the brewing process creates layers of refreshing flavors and opens up a world of potential tea-ingredient combinations.

Lemongrass
Green Tea

Honey-Peach
Black Tea

Summer Berry
Hibiscus Tea

Lavender Meyer Lemon
Mint Tea

Lemongrass Green Tea

⏰ *4 hours* 🥤 *30 oz*

In this infused green tea recipe we combine the earthy flavors of green tea with citrus-loaded fresh lemongrass to create an iced tea that harkens to southeast Asia.

---

30 oz of water

4 teaspoons of loose leaf green tea

1/2 cup of lemongrass stalks, chopped

---

i.   Add all ingredients to a 32 oz Mason jar.

ii. Seal and shake to combine.

iii. Refrigerate for 4 hours.

iv. Strain through a double layer of cheesecloth and serve over ice, garnishing with additional stalks of lemongrass. The tea will keep in the refrigerator for up to three days.

Honey-Peach Black Tea

⏰ *10 hours* 🥤 *20 oz*

We've got a soft spot for peaches, so when peaches are in season you'll find us using them in everything, including this black tea.

---

20 oz of water

3 tablespoons of loose leaf black tea

1 fresh peach, peeled and cut in thick slices

2 tablespoons of honey

---

i.   Add water, tea, and peach to a 32 oz Mason jar.

ii. Seal and shake to combine.

iii. Refrigerate for 10 hours.

iv. Strain through a double layer of cheesecloth. Add honey, reseal, and shake to combine. Serve over ice, garnishing with additional fresh peaches. The tea will keep in the refrigerator for up to three days.

Summer Berry Hibiscus Tea

⏰ 6 hours   🥤 24 oz

One of the best things about summer is the abundance of fresh fruit. We give juicy strawberries, raspberries, and blueberries a good home in this hibiscus tea.

---

24 oz of water

3 tablespoons of loose leaf hibiscus tea

5 strawberries

1/2 cup of raspberries

1/2 cup of blueberries

---

i.   Add all ingredients to a 32 oz Mason jar.

ii.   Seal and shake to combine.

iii.   Refrigerate for 6 hours.

iv.   Strain through a double layer of cheesecloth and serve over ice, garnishing with additional fresh berries. The tea will keep in the refrigerator for up to three days.

Lavender Meyer Lemon Mint Tea

⏰ 10 hours   🥤 30 oz

This hydrating and refreshingly floral iced mint tea is equally suited to a lazy afternoon outdoors or a long day at the office.

---

30 oz of water

8 sprigs of fresh mint

4 sprigs of dried lavender

4 strips of Meyer lemon zest

---

i.   Add all ingredients to a 32 oz Mason jar.

ii.   Seal and shake to combine.

iii.   Refrigerate for 10 hours.

iv.   Strain through a double layer of cheesecloth and serve over ice, garnishing with additional strips of Meyer lemon zest and lavender sprigs. The tea will keep in the refrigerator for up to three days.

Mint

Pineapple

Coconut Water

we like to use 100% raw coconut water that's never been
heat pasteurized, so it maintains its pure flavor

10 pieces of fresh pineapple, peeled

4 sprigs of fresh mint

28 oz of raw coconut water

---

i.   Combine the pineapple and mint sprigs in a 32 oz Mason jar and muddle until thoroughly crushed.

ii.   Add the coconut water, seal, and shake for 30 seconds to combine.

iii. Strain through cheesecloth, squeezing out any excess liquid.

iv.   Serve over ice. The infusion will keep in the refrigerator for up to 24 hours.

Great for postworkout hydration or hanging with friends on a sunny day.

---

keep it raw

Pay attention to what coconut water you use for this recipe. Many brands are heat pasteurized, a process that dulls the flavors. You'll want to stick with the raw, unpasteurized version, which is as close to actually cracking open a coconut as you can get.

Pineapple mint
Coconut Water

⏱ *Immediate*   🥛 *28 oz*

Coconut water in its pure, raw form is simply delicious, but the flavored varieties that you'll find at the store taste stale and lifeless. Instead of settling for something subpar, we upgrade the good stuff with tropical pineapple and cool mint to create this fresh, hydrating infusion.

Sea Salt

Lime Zest

Lime

Water

Agave

finely grating the zest from fresh limes
releases essential oils into this salted lime syrup

Salted Lime Syrup

⏱ *12 hours* 🥛 *16 oz*

Inspired by the salty lime sodas commonly found at roadside stands in Thailand, this syrup infusion is the perfect addition to carbonated water. In many Asian cuisines it's common to make drinks savory through the addition of salt, a flavor combination that wakes up your taste buds.

Zest of 4 limes

3 oz of agave syrup

1 & 1/2 teaspoons of sea salt

8 oz of water

5 oz of fresh lime juice

---

i.   Combine the lime zest, agave syrup, and sea salt in a 32 oz Mason jar.

ii.   Meanwhile, boil the water and add to the jar, stirring to combine.

iii.   Let cool to room temperature and add the lime juice. Refrigerate for 12 hours.

iv.   Strain through cheesecloth. To serve, combine 1 tablespoon of syrup with 6 oz of seltzer over ice, stir and garnish with a lime.

Great for adding to cocktails (see page 165 for a spiked salted lime soda).

---

salty vs. sweet

Salt may sound like an odd ingredient for a sweet syrup, but it actually adds a new flavor dimension to limeade and soda water that keeps you coming back for one more sip.

weeknight delivery

Prik Nam Pla
Page 43

Like every good New Yorker, weeknights at home often find us ordering in. For us, our go-to is Thai food, and we've discovered that a few infusions—spicy chili-fueled hot sauce, spiked salted lime soda—magically upgrade the whole meal from standard delivery to a truly satisfying dinner. Still hungry? Mix up a batch of popcorn topped with a sweet and spicy sriracha infused butter, put on a movie, and enjoy a great night in.

ESTD 1941 THAILAND

Mekhong

THE SPIRIT
IMPORTED OF THAILAND

Distilled Blended & Bottled by
BANGYIKHAN DISTILLERY
Product of Thailand

Neutral spirits distilled from 95% cane and 5% rice
with herbs and spices and caramel added

0ml

Spiked
Salted Lime
Soda
with Thai Mekhong

✗ *Makes one cocktail*

This effervescent cocktail combines Salted Lime Syrup with fresh lime juice, club soda, and a Thai spirit called Mekhong (which is similar to a rum and is infused with herbs and spices). If you can't find Mekhong, this recipe also works well with a high-quality white rum.

1 & 1/2 oz of Thai Mekhong (or white rum)

1 & 1/2 oz of Salted Lime Syrup (page 161)

3/4 oz of fresh lime juice

Club soda

1 slice of lime

---

i.   Add the spirits, Salted Lime Syrup, and lime juice to a Collins glass.

ii.   Add ice to the glass and fill with club soda.

iii.   Garnish with slice of lime.

spiked.

Movie Night
Page 55

the End.

we wanted to say
thanks!

Eric: There are so many people who deserve credit for their help on this project, but, with limited space, I want to thank a few in particular... To my parents: Thank you for not only listening to my crazy ideas, but encouraging me to pursue them. I learned everything I know about perseverance and persistence from you. To our friends: At this point, y'all are old hats at being hand models, taste testers, and sounding boards for our (sometimes harebrained) ideas. We can't thank you enough for your help and enthusiasm. We'll make it up to you someday (and not just with a copy of this book). To Bianca: Words can't sum up how grateful I am for your patience, insight, and support. You're there through it all, and you just keep adding to every project we tackle. "Better half" doesn't even begin to describe it. Thank you for everything. To Josh: When I showed up to that first day of college with nothing more than a duffle bag and a few dreams, little did I know that the kid across the room with the stack of cookbooks next to his bed (and a bottle of peach bourbon under it) would become my lifelong friend and business partner. Cheers to shooting for the moon, and having a good time doing it.

Josh: To my parents: Thank you for instilling and supporting my passion for cooking and food, and for funding my obscenely expensive cookbook-buying habit for so many years. Hopefully my time spent away from college at culinary school now actually makes some sense. To Eric: Thanks for being the best business partner, friend, and hand model I could ever hope for (your nails look great by the way...did you get a manicure?). To Bianca: Thank you for transforming our attempts at writing into what you read today in this book. You are a truly talented editor. To our friends who gave their time, advice, and support for free: Thank you (a special thanks to a certain Australian silverware hunter, you're the best). To Rebecca: Thank you for being my sounding board and tremendously patient better half. Your support and advice made this book what it is today. Thank you for putting up with so many late nights and crowded refrigerators packed with strange looking Mason jars labeled with things like "ROAST-PINE-MEZ // DO NOT OPEN." Thanks for not opening that. And an even bigger thanks for tasting it when I did.

Eric & Josh: To our friends who generously provided hours of their time and heaps of valuable feedback, thank you (you know who you are). A big thank you to our W&P team: Justin for being a design wizard, Jessica for being a true wordsmith, and Jordan for just being so damn good-looking. You guys rock. Last but not least, thank you to Elizabeth Tilton for being the raddest pastry-cooking, food-event-throwing, beer-shotgunning, foreword-writing friend two guys could ask for.

index.

Published in the United States by Clarkson Potter/Publishers, an imprint of the
Crown Publishing Group, a division of Penguin Random House LLC, New York.
www.crownpublishing.com
www.clarksonpotter.com

CLARKSON POTTER is a trademark and POTTER with colophon is a registered
trademark of Penguin Random House LLC.

Library of Congress Cataloging-in-Publication Data
Prum, Eric.
Infuse : water, spirit, oil / Eric Prum, Josh Williams.
1. Pickled foods. 2 Cooking (Oils and fats)
3. Cooking (Spices) I. Williams, Josh. II. Title.

TX805.P78 2015
641.4'62--dc23

ISBN 978-0-8041-8676-6
eISBN 978-0-8041-8677-3

Printed in Hong Kong

Book and cover design by W&P Design
Cover photograph by W&P Design
www.wandpdesign.com

For more recipes and to purchase the tools used in *Infuse*,
visit us online at www.masonshaker.com

10 9 8 7 6 5 4 3

First Edition